It's fun to draw
Robots
and
Aliens

Mark Bergin

Author:

Mark Bergin was born in Hastings, England. He has illustrated an award winning series and written over twenty books. He has designed many books, layouts and storyboards in many styles, including cartoon, for numerous books, posters and adverts. He lives in Bexhill-on-Sea with his wife and three children.

Editorial Assistant:
Rob Walker

HOW TO USE THIS BOOK:

Start by following the numbered splats on the left hand page. These steps will ask you to add some lines to your drawing. The new lines are always drawn in red so you can see how the drawing builds from step to step. Read the 'You can do it!' splats to learn about drawing and colouring techniques you can use.

Published in Great Britain in MMXII by
Book House, an imprint of
The Salariya Book Company Ltd
25 Marlborough Place, Brighton BN1 1UB
www.salariya.com
www.book-house.co.uk

ISBN-13: 978-1-907184-71-0

PAPER FROM
SUSTAINABLE
FORESTS

Visit our website at **www.book-house.co.uk**
or go to **www.salariya.com** for **free** electronic versions of:
You Wouldn't Want to be an Egyptian Mummy!
You Wouldn't Want to be a Roman Gladiator!
You Wouldn't Want to be a Polar Explorer!
You Wouldn't Want to Sail on a 19th-Century Whaling Ship!

Visit our BookHouse100 channel to see Mark Bergin doing
step by step illustrations:

www.youtube.com/user/bookhouse100

Contents

Klank, a robot

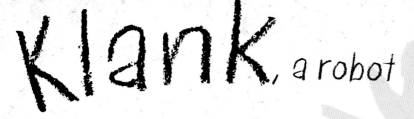

1 Draw a rectangle for the head. Add mouth, ears and dots for the eyes.

2 Draw the neck and a rectangle for the body.

you can do it!

Use black felt-tip for the lines and add colour using coloured felt-tips.

3 Draw in the legs. Add circles for the knee joints.

4 Add the arms and hands, with circles at the elbow joints.

splat-a-fact!
Robots have very
good memories and
are good at maths.

Claude, an alien

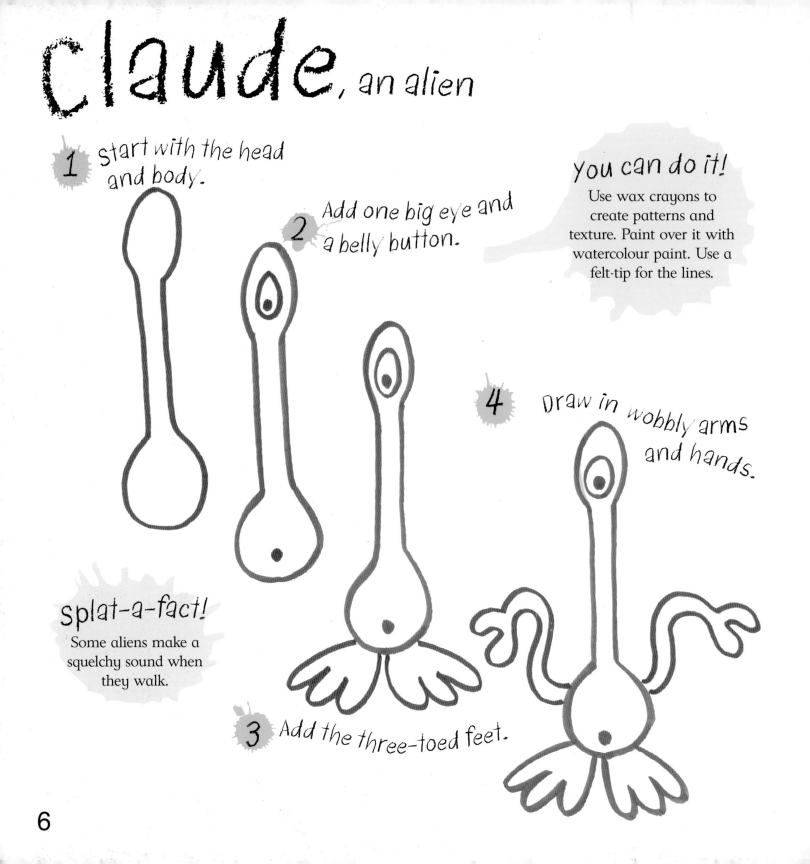

1 Start with the head and body.

2 Add one big eye and a belly button.

3 Add the three-toed feet.

4 Draw in wobbly arms and hands.

you can do it!
Use wax crayons to create patterns and texture. Paint over it with watercolour paint. Use a felt-tip for the lines.

splat-a-fact!
Some aliens make a squelchy sound when they walk.

spike, an alien

you can do it!
Use a dark pencil to draw the outline and add colour with watercolour paint.

1 Start with a spiky shape for the head.

2 Add a smiley mouth and four dots for eyes.

splat-a-fact!
There are no 'Alien Olympics' - it wouldn't be fair as some aliens have lots of legs.

4 Add five legs and feet.

3 Draw in the skin patterns.

8

Bob the blob,
an alien

1 Start with the body.

2 Draw in two big feet.

splat-a-fact!
Aliens only have one eye... or sometimes two... or maybe even six or ten...

3 Add the antennae with eyes.

4 Draw in one big eye and a mouth.

10

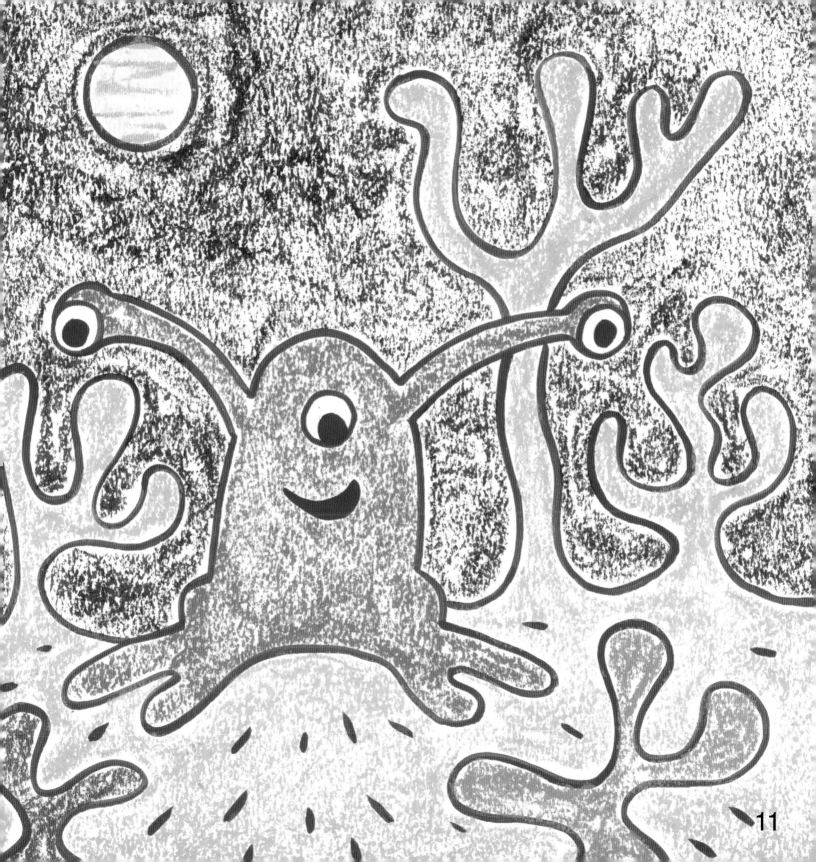

11

Rivet, a robot

1 Start with a circle for the body. Draw a line near the top and add details.

2 Add the mouth and dots for eyes.

3 Draw in the legs and feet with circles and half circles.

you can do it!

Use a black felt-tip for the lines. Add colour by dabbing on paint with a sponge.

4 Draw in a glass helmet.

5 Add circles for the arms. Draw in the hands.

splat-a-fact!

Robots don't think - they just know what to do next.

Grabbit, a robot

1 Tear out the head and body shapes. Stick the body down. Stick the head down. Add a mouth, a line and dots for the eyes.

2 Tear out the shape for the flashing light. Stick down.

splat-a-fact!
Robots have complicated circuits and about 54 metres of wire inside them.

you can do it!
Tear out the robot's shapes from coloured paper. Stick these to a sheet of coloured paper. Use a felt-tip for the face and flashing light.

3 Tear out shapes for the legs and feet. Stick down.

4 Tear out shapes for the arms, hands and a red gem. Stick down.

15

Octo, an alien

1 Start with a big oval for the head and a small oval for the body. Draw two lines for the neck.

2 Add the ears, mouth and dots for the eyes.

you can do it!
Use coloured pastel pencils and blend and smudge the colours with your finger. Draw the lines with felt-tip.

3 Draw in four legs and feet.

Splat-a-fact!
Four-armed aliens can blow their nose, eat dinner, do homework and scratch their ear - all at the same time.

4 Add four arms, each with a three-fingered hand.

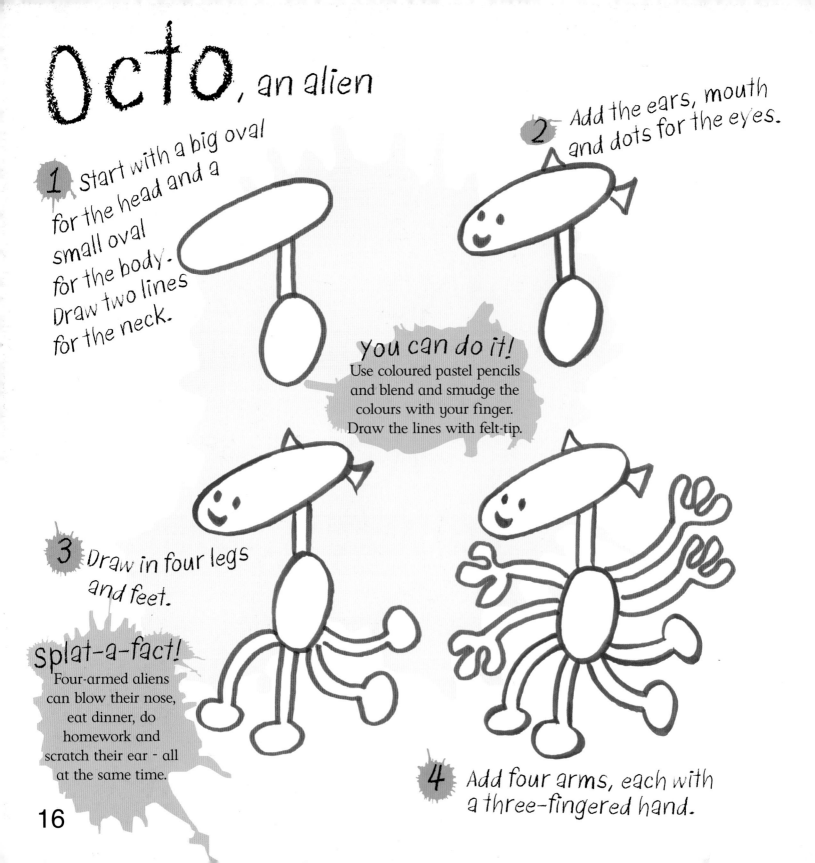

16

Rover, a robot

1 Start with a big half-circle for the head. Add ears, mouth and dots for the eyes.

2 Add the shape of the tracks. Join the tracks to the head.

you can do it!
Use wax crayons for texture and paint over it with watercolour paint. Use felt-tip for the lines.

3 Add lines and circles to the tracks.

4 Draw in the arms and antennae.

Martian Mike, an alien

1 Start with a triangular shape for the head, add the small round body and neck.

2 Add the eyes, mouth and antennae.

you can do it!
Use wax crayons to create texture and paint over it with watercolour paint. Use felt-tip for the lines.

Splat-a-fact!
Some aliens live to be 3,967,000 years old.

3 Add the legs and feet.

4 Draw in the arms and hands.

20

Rusty, a robot

1 Draw a circle for the head, adding the eyes and mouth.

2 Add the body and the neck.

you can do it!
Use black felt-tip for the lines and use different colours of felt-tips to colour in.

splat-a-fact!
Unhappy robots close down their circuitry - their lights go out and they come to a stop.

4 Draw in the arms and hands. Add circles at the elbow and wrist joints.

3 Draw the leg and feet shapes. Add circles at the knee joints.

5 Finish off the head.

23

Zango, an alien

1 Start with an oval for the body. Add five antennae.

2 Add five eyes and a mouth.

you can do it!
Use black felt-tip for the lines. Colour in using coloured pencils.

Splat-a-fact!
Aliens never wear glasses. If one eye goes wonky they've usually got plenty of other eyes to use.

3 Draw in six legs and feet using curved lines and half-circles.

4 Add a big half-circle for the flying saucer. Add details.

Zakk, an alien

1 Start with ovals for the head and body. Add the neck.

2 Draw in ears, mouth and five eyes.

you can do it!

Use a felt-tip for the lines. Add colour using oil pastels in a scribbly way so the colour looks more interesting.

splat-a-fact!

Aliens do not live on Earth - the weather is too changeable.

3 Draw in the legs with curvy lines.

4 Add two tentacle arms with curvy lines.

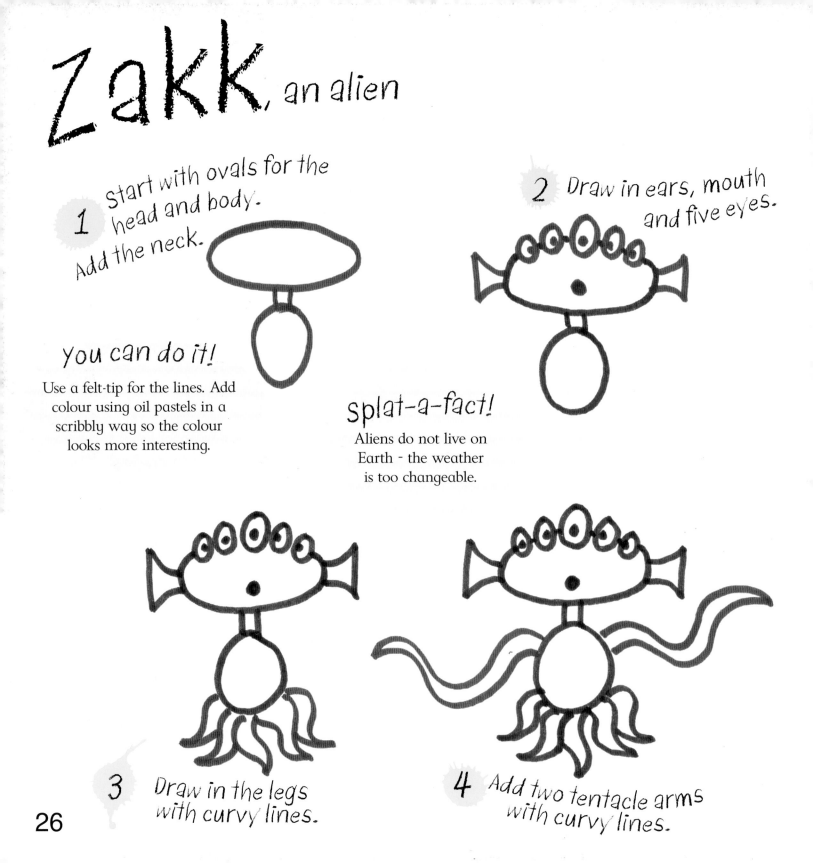

26

Mega-klank, a robot

Cut out a rectangle for the head. Stick down. Draw in the eyes and mouth.

Cut out rectangles for the body and neck. Stick down the neck then the body.

You can do it!
Cut out the robot shapes from coloured paper. Stick these on to a sheet of blue paper as shown. Use felt-tip for the lines.

Cut out the leg shapes. Stick down. Add a felt-tip line. Cut out foot shapes. Stick down.

Cut out the shapes of the arms. Stick down. Cut out shapes for details. Stick down.

MAKE SURE YOU GET AN ADULT TO HELP YOU WHEN USING SCISSORS!

splat-a-fact!
Robots don't need sleep.

29

whizz-pop, a robot

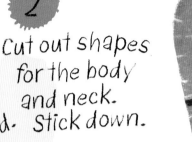

2 Cut out shapes for the body and neck. Stick down.

1 Cut out the shape of the head. Stick down. Add the eyes and mouth with a marker pen.

MAKE SURE YOU GET AN ADULT TO HELP YOU WHEN USING SCISSORS!

You can do it!

Cut out the robot shapes from tin foil. Stick these onto a sheet of black paper. Use a marker pen for the lines. Add paint splatters and torn paper for the background.

3 Cut out shapes for the feet and the head details. Add lines with a marker pen.

4 Cut out shapes for the arms and hands. Stick down. Add circles at the joints with a marker pen.

Index

www.salariya.com
where books come to life!

Download our free iPhone and iPad catalogue app. Search for Salariya or Book House

Available on the App Store

Follow us on Facebook and Twitter

www.youtube.com/user/BookHouse100

Scribblers
Bright Start
fiction
Fiction for children and teenagers

FREE WEB BOOK!
Free activities, puzzles and web books, with information about our books for babies, toddlers and pre-school

Children's non-fiction and graphic novels

THE BOOK HOUSE BLOG
The Book House blog – competitions, giveaways and current news

Dead?
Four free web books

FREE WEB BOOKS!